# DEAR · · · · · · · · · · · · · · · · · · · · · · · · · · ·

· · · · · · · · · · · · · · · · · · · · · · · · · · · · · · · · · ·

· · · · · · · · · · · · · · · · · · · · · · · · · · · · · · · · · ·

· · · · · · · · · · · · · · · · · · · · · · · · · · · · · · · · · ·

# FROM · · · · · · · · · · · · · · · · · · · · · · · · · ·

Q: WHAT DO YOU CALL 2 PIECES OF TOAST THAT ARE ZOMBIFIED?

A: THE UN-BREAD & THE WALKING DEAD BREAD.

THIS CHRISTMAS I AM BUYING MY WIFE A PROSTHETIC LEG.

NOT AS HER MAIN GIFT, JUST A STOCKING FILLER.

My English lit teacher told me I would never be good at poetry because I'm dyslexic.
But look at me now, I've made four plates, three vases and a jug!

Q: Why did the poor old chap fall into a well?

A: He couldn't see that well.

Q: What did Santa say to Mrs Claus while he was watching the weather report?

A: Looks like reindeer.

I was asked to go out by four women today.

It turns out I was in the female changing rooms.

DAVE THREW A BIG GLASS
BOTTLE OF OMEGA 3 PILLS AT
ME.
NO NEED TO WORRY! I ONLY
SUFFERED SUPER FISH OIL
INJURIES.

DAVE: I DON'T UNDERSTAND
WHAT CLONING IS.

ME: THAT MAKES 2 OF US.

Q: How much room do
fungi need to grow?

A: As mushroom as possible.

Q: What do you call a
knight who is petrified
of fighting?

A: Sir Render.

HAVE YOU HEARD ABOUT DAVE? HE'S DESIGNED AN INVISIBLE AEROPLANE.

I CAN'T SEE IT TAKING OFF.

Q: WHAT DO YOU CALL A MOUSE THAT CONSTANTLY SWEARS?

A: A CURSOR.

WORKING AT AN
UNEMPLOYMENT OFFICE MUST
BE SO ANNOYING.

EVEN IF YOU GET FIRED YOU
STILL HAVE TO COME IN THE
NEXT DAY.

ME: "EXCUSE ME WHERE
ARE THE ARNOLD
SCHWARZENEGGER ACTION
FIGURES?"
STORE CLERK: "AISLE B,
BACK."

Q: What's the difference between a badly dressed meerkat on a tricycle and a well-dressed meerkat on a bicycle?

A: Attire.

A cop pulled me over last night and said: "Papers."

I shouted "scissors" and drove off.

Q: What do you call a bee
that was born in America?

A: A USB.

This Christmas, I am
getting my children an
alarm clock that swears at
them rather than ringing.
They're in a for a rude
awakening.

BUT THE RECIPE SAID, "SET THE OVEN TO 180 DEGREES." NOW I CAN'T OPEN THE OVEN AS THE DOOR FACES THE WALL.

I ACCIDENTALLY RUBBED KETCHUP IN MY EYES.

NOW I HAVE HEINZSIGHT.

Q: What is the main
difference between
ignorance & indifference?

A: I don't know, and I
don't care.

My Manager is threatening
to fire the employee with
the worst posture.

I have a hunch it might be
me.

UNFORTUNATELY, SUPERMAN
WON'T BE ABLE TO FIGHT THE
EVIL VAMPIRE THIS EVENING.

HE WON'T GO NEAR THE
CRYPT TONIGHT.

I ALWAYS KNOCK 3 TIMES ON
THE FRIDGE BEFORE I OPEN
IT.

JUST IN CASE THERE'S A
SALAD DRESSING.

Q: WHAT SOUNDS JUST LIKE A SNEEZE AND IS MADE OF LEATHER?

A: A SHOE.

THREE CONSPIRACY THEORISTS WALK INTO A BAR.

YOU CAN NOT TELL ME THAT'S JUST A COINCIDENCE!

I WANT TO TELL YOU A
STORY ABOUT A GIRL WHO
ONLY EATS PLANTS.

YOU'VE PROBABLY NEVER
HEARD OF HERBIVORE.

I HAD THE MOST RANDOM &
CRAZIEST DREAM LAST
NIGHT, I WEIGHED LESS
THAN A THOUSANDTH OF A
GRAM.

I WAS LIKE OMG.

DAVE TOLD ME I MAKE
PEOPLE UNCOMFORTABLE BY
NOT RESPECTING THEIR
PERSONAL SPACE. I WAS UPSET
BY HIS COMMENTS,
IT COMPLETELY RUINED
OUR BATH.

I BOILED A FUNNY BONE
LAST WEEK.

IT TURNED INTO A
LAUGHING STOCK.

DAVE: MY GREAT UNCLES
LAST WORDS WERE "PINTS!
LITRES! & GALLONS"

ME: WOW THAT REALLY
SPEAKS VOLUMES.

I WENT TO VISIT MY BEST
FRIENDS NEW HOUSE. HE
TOLD ME TO RELAX AND
MAKE MYSELF AT HOME.
SO, I THREW HIM OUT.
I CAN'T STAND VISITORS.

I arrived an hour early at the restaurant last night.
Manager: "Do you mind waiting for a bit?"
Me: "No, not at all"
Manager: "Great, take the Pad Thai to table 5

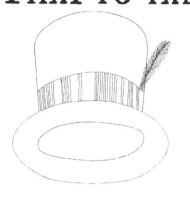

Q: What do you call a can opener that's broken?

A: A can't opener.

TOO MANY PEOPLE ARE
JUDGEMENTAL THESE DAYS.

I CAN TELL JUST BY LOOKING
AT THEM.

I GOT ARRESTED LAST
NIGHT FOR ILLEGALLY
DOWNLOADING THE WHOLE
OF WIKIPEDIA.

I TOLD THEM I COULD
EXPLAIN EVERYTHING.

I GOT FIRED WHEN I ASKED A CUSTOMER IF THEY PREFERRED SMOKING OR NON-SMOKING. APPARENTLY, THE POLITICALLY CORRECT TERMS ARE "CREMATION" AND BURIAL".

EVERYONE IS USUALLY SHOCKED WHEN THEY FIND OUT I AM NOT A VERY GOOD ELECTRICIAN.

My wife told me to take the spider out rather than killing him. So we went out, had a couple of drinks, nice little chap. He's a web designer.

If I had to penny for every time I had no idea with what was going on, I would be like, why am I always getting this free money?

How have I only just
found out that
"Aarrghhh" is not a real
word?

I can't express how angry
I am.

Q: What do you call a pig
with three eyes?

A: Piiig.

As I was leaving the elevator, the attendant said: "see you later son". I told him not to call me son as he wasnt my dad! to which he replied, "maybe not, but who brought you up?"

Dave says I'm getting fat. In my defence...

I have had a lot on my plate recently.

Q: WHAT DO YOU CALL A JAVELIN THROWER WHO IS NERVOUS?

A: SHAKESPEARE.

EVERYONE AT OUR WEDDING CRIED.

EVEN OUR WEDDING CAKE WAS IN TIERS.

HAVE YOU HEARD ABOUT THE
MATHEMATICIAN WHO IS
TERRIFIED OF NEGATIVE
NUMBERS?

HE WILL STOP AT NOTHING
TO AVOID THEM.

I AM GOING CRAZY I HAVE
FORGOTTEN HOW TO WRITE 1,
1000, 51, 6 AND 500 IN
ROMAN NUMERALS.

I M LIVID

IF YOU EVER FEEL DOWN,
TRY DRINKING A GALLON OF
WATER BEFORE AT 11PM.

THAT WILL GIVE YOU A
REASON TO GET UP IN THE
MORNING.

Q: WHAT DO YOU CALL AN
APOLOGY LETTER WRITTEN
ONLY IN DOTS AND DASHES?

A: RE-MORSE CODE.

SON: "DADDY, CAN YOU EXPLAIN TO ME WHAT A SOLAR ECLIPSE IS?"

DAD: No. SUN.

DOCTOR: "WOULD YOU LIKE THE GOOD NEWS OR BAD NEWS FIRST?"
ME: GOOD NEWS PLEASE!
DOCTOR: "WE'RE NAMING A DISEASE AFTER YOU."

I CAN'T STAND IT WHEN
PEOPLE DON'T KNOW THE
DIFFERENCE BETWEEN YOU
AND YOU'RE!!

THERE SO STUPID.

Q: WHAT HAPPENS WHEN
YOU PUT A DUCK IN A
CEMENT MIXER?

A: QUACKS IN THE
PAVEMENT.

I'M ASSUMING BECAUSE OF LOCKDOWN WE'LL ONLY BE MAKING INSIDE JOKES FROM NOW ON?

MY KIDS WERE A BIT SCARED OF EATING THEIR TOAST THIS HALLOWEEN MORNING. I TOLD THEM NOT TO BE SILLY BECAUSE WE AIN'T AFRAID OF NO TOAST!

I JUST GOT A JOB AT A COMPANY THAT MAKES BICYCLE WHEELS!

I'M THE SPOKESPERSON.

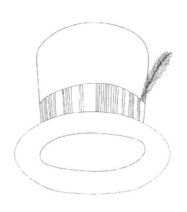

I'M MAKING A NEW SERIES ON HOW TO FLY A PLANE.

WE'RE CURRENTLY FILMING THE PILOT.

Dave: Your wife and daughter look like identical twins!
Me: I know! They were separated at birth.

Q: What has 4 wheels and flies?

A: A garbage truck.

I WAS FEELING DOWN ABOUT THE FUTURE TODAY; MY MATE RECOMMENDED I INSTALL THE NEW VERSION OF OFFICE. IT HAS DEFINITELY IMPROVED MY OUTLOOK!

I HAVE FINALLY FINISHED WRITING MY FIRST BOOK; IT'S ABOUT FALLING DOWN A STAIRCASE.

IT'S A STEP BY STEP GUIDE.

DID I TELL YOU ABOUT THE BAND I WAS IN IN 1985, WE WERE CALLED THE PREVENTION.

WE WERE SO MUCH BETTER THAN THE CURE.

Q: WHAT ARE RETIRED TERMINATORS CALLED?

A: EXTERMINATORS.

I TOLD MY WIFE THAT
HUSBANDS LIKE ME AGE LIKE
FINE WINE, WE JUST GET
BETTER WITH AGE.

SHE AGREED AND THEN
LOCKED ME IN THE CELLAR.

Q: WHAT DO YOU CALL A KID
WITH GINGER HAIR WHO'S
FANTASTIC AT MARTIAL ARTS?

A: THE CARROTY KID.

Q: WHAT SUBJECT DOES A
WITCH TEACH AT SCHOOL?

A: SPELLING.

Q: WHY DO BEES ALWAYS
HAVE STICKY HAIR?

A: THEY USE HONEYCOMBS.

WHEN I WAS 10 MY MOM TOLD ME TO GO TO THE PARK WITH MY BROTHER SO SHE COULD SET UP HIS SURPRISE BIRTHDAY PARTY.
THAT IS WHEN I REALIZED HE WAS HER FAVORITE TWIN.

MY WIFE GOT ME A DRONE FOR MY BIRTHDAY. I GOT IT STUCK UP A TREE, ITS ACTUALLY NOT THE WORST THING THAT HAPPENED TO ME TODAY.
BUT IT'S DEFINITELY UP THERE.

Q: WHICH FRIENDS ENJOY GOING OUT FOR DINNER WITH YOU THE MOST?

A: YOUR TASTE BUDS.

Q: WHY DID THE STAR WARS MOVIES COME OUT 4 5 6 1 2 3?

A: IN CHARGE OF THE SCHEDULING. YODA WAS.

My mate Dave can't afford to pay his water bill anymore, so I sent him a card, "Get well soon."

My wife always says I only have 2 faults.

I never listen — and something else...

I WARNED MY KIDS ABOUT USING THEIR WHISTLE INDOORS & GAVE THEM ONE LAST CHANCE.

UNFORTUNATELY, THEY BLEW IT.

Q: WHAT DID 2 SAY TO 3 WHEN THEY SAW 6 ACT LIKE AN IDIOT?

A: DON'T PAY ANY ATTENTION TO HIM. HE'S JUST A PRODUCT OF OUR TIMES.

A MUMMY HAS JUST BEEN
DISCOVERED IN EGYPT. IT
WAS FOUND COVERED IN
CHOCOLATE AND NUTS.

THEY BELIEVE HE WAS
CALLED PHARAOH ROCHER!

I WAS ARRESTED LAST NIGHT
FOR IMPERSONATING A
POLITICIAN.

I WAS LITERALLY JUST SITTING
THERE DOING NOTHING.

Q: WHAT HAPPENED TO THE WOODEN CAR THAT HAD A WOODEN ENGINE AND WOODEN WHEELS?

A: IT WOODEN START.

Q: WHAT DO YOU CALL A BEAT-UP BATMAN?

A: BRUISED WAYNE.

I SAW ON THE NEWS THAT
SOME GUY HAS BEEN STEALING
WHEELS OFF POLICE CARS.

DON'T WORRY; THE POLICE
ARE WORKING TIRELESSLY TO
CATCH HIM.

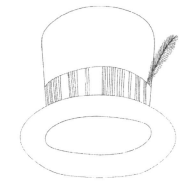

YOU'VE REALLY GOTTA
HAND IT TO SHORT PEOPLE.

BECAUSE THEY USUALLY
CAN'T REACH IT.

I WAS SITTING DRINKING
COFFEE IN MY SLIPPERS THIS
MORNING, THEN I THOUGHT
TO MYSELF...

I REALLY SHOULD WASH SOME
MUGS.

SUNDAYS ARE ALWAYS A
LITTLE BIT SAD,
BUT..
THE DAY BEFORE IS ALWAYS A
SADDER DAY.

I WAS IN AN UBER EARLIER & THE DRIVER SAID, "I LOVE MY JOB BECAUSE I AM MY OWN BOSS & NOBODY TELLS ME WHAT TO DO."
THEN I SAID:
"TURN LEFT HERE."

DELOREAN FOR SALE. GOOD SHAPE, LOW MILEAGE... ONLY DRIVEN FROM TIME TO TIME.

IT'S OUR WEDDING
ANNIVERSARY TODAY. MY
WIFE AND I HAVE BEEN
HAPPILY MARRIED FOR TWO
YEARS NOW.
2001 AND 2016.

MY PUPPY MINTON HAS
EATEN ALL OF THE
SHUTTLECOCKS!

BAD MINTON.

DAVE: WHAT YOU DOING
THIS WEEKEND?
ME: I'M GOING TO BUY
GLASSES.
DAVE: AND THEN?
ME: THEN I'LL SEE.

Q: WHAT DO YOU CALL A
LAUGHING MOTORCYCLE?

A: YAMAHAHA.

I ASKED MY WIFE WHAT SHE WANTED FOR HER BIRTHDAY. SHE SAID: "NOTHING WOULD MAKE ME HAPPIER THAN A DIAMOND NECKLACE."

SO I GOT HER NOTHING.

THE DOCTOR SAID I HAVE A CHRONIC FEAR OF GIANTS.

IT'S CALLED FEEFIPHOBIA.

4 MEN ARE ON A BOAT WITH 5 CIGARETTES, THEY HAVE NOTHING TO LIGHT THEM WITH.

THEY THROW 1 CIGARETTE OVERBOARD, AND THE BOAT BECOMES A CIGARETTE LIGHTER.

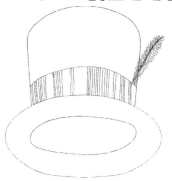

THE DETECTIVE FIGURED OUT WHO THE MURDERER WAS WITHIN MINUTES.

IT WAS A BRIEF CASE.

EVERY TOM, DICK AND HARRY KNOWS WHERE THE BIG APPLE IS BUT DOES ANYONE KNOW WHERE THE MINNEAPOLIS?

I JUST SAW ONE OF THE WORKERS AT WALMART SCAN THE EYES OF A RUDE CUSTOMER WITH THEIR BARCODE READER. YOU SHOULD HAVE SEEN THE LOOK ON HIS FACE, PRICELESS.

I QUIT MY JOB AS AN AMAZON
DELIVERY DRIVER AS SOON AS
THEY HANDED ME THE FIRST
BOX.
I LOOKED AT IT & JUST
THOUGHT: "THIS ISN'T FOR
ME."

I PUT UP AN ELECTRIC
FENCE AROUND MY
PROPERTY THIS MORNING.

MY NEIGHBOUR IS DEAD
AGAINST IT.

Q: WHY DO WE PRONOUNCE "QUEUE" AS "Q"?

A: BECAUSE THE OTHER LETTERS ARE WAITING IN LINE.

MY WIFE LEFT ME BECAUSE I AM INSECURE.

OH NO WAIT! SHE'S BACK. SHE JUST WENT TO MAKE A CUP OF TEA.

ME & MY WIFE ENJOY SETTING
THINGS ON FIRE. SO DOES OUR
CHILD. AFTER HE SET FIRE
TO HIS FIRST BUILDING ME &
MY WIFE LOOKED AT EACH
OTHER & SAID PROUDLY
"YEP, THAT'S ARSON."

THE OLD SAYING IS CORRECT;
JUSTICE IS A DISH BEST
SERVED COLD.
BECAUSE IF IT WAS SERVED
WARM, IT WOULD BE
JUSTWATER.

I WENT TO THE DOCTOR
WITH HEARING PROBLEMS.
HE ASKED "CAN YOU
DESCRIBE THE SYSMTOMS?"
I REPLIED "HOMER'S A FAT
LAZY DUDE WITH 3 KIDS & A
WIFE WITH TALL BLUE HAIR."

I'VE STARTED INVESTING IN
STOCKS.
MAINLY BEEF, CHICKEN &
VEG. I WILL BECOME A
BOUILLONAIRE ONE DAY.

EVERY MORNING SINCE NEW
YEARS DAY, I ANNOUNCE
LOUDLY TO MY FAMILY THAT
I'M GOING FOR A JOG, AND
THEN I DON'T.
IT'S MY LONGEST-RUNNING
JOKE THIS YEAR.

Q: WHAT'S THE BEST THING
TO SAY TO YOUR SISTER
WHEN SHE'S CRYING?

A: ARE YOU HAVING A
CRISIS?

Q: What do you call a polite woman who builds bridges?

A: A civil engineer.

Q: What's orange and sounds like a parrot?

A: A carrot.

Q: WHAT WILL HAPPEN IF YOU CUT OFF YOUR LEFT ARM?

A: YOUR RIGHT ARM WILL BE LEFT.

Q: WHAT IS THE BEST WAY TO GET ATTENTION FROM YOUR WIFE?

A: SIT DOWN AND LOOK COMFORTABLE.

RUSSIAN DOLLS REALLY
ANNOY ME.

THEY ARE JUST SO FULL OF
THEMSELVES.

Q: WHAT DO YOU CALL A
POTATO WEARING GLASSES?

A: A SPECTATER.

Q: WHY CAN'T YOU BREED AN
EEL WITH AN EAGLE?

A: IT'S EELEAGLE.

AS I STARTED TO REVERSE,
I THOUGHT TO MYSELF...

"THIS TAKES ME BACK."

Q: What do you call a little girl who's half French and half Scottish?

A: A oui lass.

Therapist: Your wife is upset because you never buy her flowers?
Me: To be completely honest, I had no idea my wife sold flowers.

Q: What training or qualifications does a garbage collector need?

A: None. They just pick it up as they go.

Q: What does a house always wear?

A: Address.

THE PUPPY SWALLOWED A
LOAD OF SCRABBLE TILES.

THE NEXT POOP COULD
SPELL DISASTER.

I WENT INTO THE SHOP AND
ASKED FOR 14 BEES. THE
OWNER HANDED ME 15.
"OH, THERES ONE TOO MANY
HERE" I SAID.
"THAT ONE IS A FREEBIE."
SHE REPLIED.

Q: What's the most
challenging part of being
a vegan?

A: Keeping it to yourself.

My son told me I can't
use "beefstew" as my
apple id password.

Apparently, it's not
stroganoff.

I BOUGHT SOME PANTS THAT KEPT PICKING UP STATIC ELECTRICITY, SO I DECIDED TO TAKE THEM BACK TO THE STORE.
I COMPLAINED & THEY GAVE ME ANOTHER ONE FREE OF CHARGE.

Q: IS A LITRE OF WATER OR A LITRE OF BUTANE HEAVIER?

A: WATER. NO MATTER HOW MUCH, BUTANE WILL ALWAYS BE A LIGHTER FLUID.

SOME OLD CHAP KNOCKED ON
THE DOOR EARLIER ASKING FOR
SMALL DONATIONS TO KEEP
THE LOCAL SWIMMING POOL
OPEN. I WAS MORE THAN HAPPY
TO HELP OUT, SO I GAVE HIM A
GLASS OF WATER.

I ASKED THE ANAESTHETIST IF
I COULD ADMINISTER MY OWN
ANAESTHETIC.
SHE SAID "OF COURSE, GO
AHEAD, KNOCK YOURSELF
OUT!"

THE BANK CALLED ME EARLIER TO LET ME KNOW I HAD AN OUTSTANDING BALANCE.
I SAID: "THANKS I USED TO DO GYMNASTICS" AND HUNG UP.

Q: WHAT TIME DOES SEAN CONNERY GET TO US OPEN?

A: TENNISH.

I GAVE MY WIFE A GLUESTICK
INSTEAD OF HER LIPSTICK.

SHE STILL ISN'T TALKING TO
ME.

Q: WHY DON'T ANTS GET
SICK?

A: BECAUSE THEY HAVE
LITTLE ANTY BODIES.

SOMEONE BROKE INTO THE
HOUSE LAST NIGHT; THEY
WERE LOOKING FOR MONEY.

SO I GOT OUT OF BED TO LOOK
WITH HIM.

I WONDER WHY DOGS CAN'T
READ AN MRI OR X-RAYS.

BUT CATSCAN.

I HAD A DREAM LAST NIGHT
THAT I WROTE LORD OF THE
RINGS.

GUESS I WAS TOLKIEN IN MY
SLEEP.

Q: WHY DOES THE LANDLORD
LET 9 ANTS LIVE IN HIS FOR
FREE?

A: BECAUSE THEY ARE NOT
TENANTS.

ME AND MY PAL DAVE SHARE
AN AMAZON ACCOUNT TO SAVE
ON SHIPPING COSTS.

MY WIFE CALLS US PRIME
MATES.

FOUR YEARS AGO MY DOCTOR
TOLD ME I WAS GOING DEAF.

I HAVEN'T HEARD FROM HIM
SINCE.

I BROKE MY FINGER TODAY.
DON'T FEEL SO GREAT.

BUT ON THE OTHER HAND, I
AM FINE.

MY MOTHER-IN-LAW HATES
HER NEW STAIRLIFT.

SHE SAYS IT DRIVES HER UP
THE WALL.

Q: WHAT WASHES UP ON TINY BEACHES?

A: MICROWAVES.

I GOT ARRESTED LAST NIGHT FOR STEALING COOKING UTENSILS.

IT WAS DEFINITELY WORTH THE WHISK.

My wife didn't believe me when I told her I accidentally glued myself to my memoir.

But that's my story and I'm sticking to it.

Whatever you do, DO NOT spell the word "part" backwards!

It's most definitely a "trap."

I TOLD MY SON TO TAKE OFF
THE SHELL OF HIS RACING
SNAIL AS IT WOULD MAKE HIM
FASTER.

I WAS WRONG; HE'S MORE
SLUGGISH NOW.

I CAN'T STAND IT WHEN
PEOPLE SAY AGE IS JUST A
NUMBER.

AGE IS CLEARLY A WORD!

My housemates are adamant the house is haunted.

I've lived here for 189 years & have not noticed anything out of the ordinary.

Q: How does a vegan start grace before their supper?

A: Lettuce pray.

MY WIFE THREATENED TO LEAVE ME BECAUSE I HAVE NO SENSE OF DIRECTION.

SO I PACKED UP MY STUFF AND RIGHT.

THE DERMATOLOGIST PRESCRIBED ME SOME ANTI-GLOATING CREAM.

I CAN'T WAIT TO RUB IT IN.

Q: WHICH APP DOES CAPTAIN HOOK HATE?

A: TIKTOK

I HAVE BEEN TRYING TO COME UP WITH A FUNNY JOKE ABOUT SOCIAL DISTANCING.

THIS IS AS CLOSE AS I COULD GET.

I JUST FOUND OUT MY
MANAGER IS ACTUALLY A
GHOST.

TO BE HONEST, I HAD MY
SUSPICIONS THE MOMENT HE
WALKED THROUGH THE DOOR.

Q: WHY WAS THE QUEEN
ONLY 12 INCHES TALL?

A: BECAUSE SHE WAS A
RULER.

Q: WHY SHOULD WE NOT LET 2020 END?

A: BECAUSE THAT WOULD BE ADMITTING THAT 2021!

THE FIRST THING I DO EVERY MORNING IS MAKE MY BED.

I WILL BE RETURNING IT TO IKEA AS SOON AS I FIND THE RECEIPT.

My wife's dad is a fisherman.

Annete was a good catch for sure.

I am reading a book on anti-gravity.

It's impossible to put down.

Q: What happens if you rearrange the letters of a POSTMAN?

A: They become VERY ANGRY.

I only ate brown bread for dinner tonight.

That was my wholemeal.

Two chickpeas are walking home from the bar when one chickpea starts to vomit. The other chickpea asks, "Are you alright?" and the chickpea answers, "No, I falafel."

Don't you just love the way the earth rotates?

It really makes my day.

I TOOK MY SON TO "TAKE YOUR KID TO WORK DAY."
HE WAS NOT IMPRESSED AND STARTED CRYING IN FRONT OF MY COLLEGUES WHILE SOBBING "WHERE ARE ALL THE CLOWNS YOU SAID YOU WORKED WITH?"

AMAZON IS USELESS SOMETIMES. I TRIED SEARCHING FOR LIGHTERS BUT ALL THEY HAD WAS 11,643 MATCHES.

RECENTLY TOOK A POLE:
TURNS OUT 99.% OF PEOPLE
WERE ANGRY WHEN THEIR
TENT COLLAPSED.

CAN YOU BELIEVE OUR
NEIGHBOUR WAS
KNOCKING ON THE DOOR
AT 3AM!

LUCKILY I WAS AWAKE
PLAYING THE BAGPIPES.

WE JUST GOT A UNIVERSAL
REMOTE.

IT REALLY CHANGES
EVERYTHING.

I DIDN'T LIKE MY BEARD
MUCH AT FIRST.

BUT THEN IT GREW ON ME.

Q: WHAT DO YOU CALL THE
AVERAGE POTATO?

A: A COMMONTATER.

MY WIFE TOLD ME I AM
TOO IMMATURE.

I TOLD HER TO GET OUT
OF MY FORT.

# Q: What did the pirate say on his 80th birthday.

## A: Aye Matey.

I came up with a new word.

## Plagiarism.

Q: Which knight invented King Arthur's Round Table?
A: Sir Cumference.

Q: Why did Adele cross the road?

A: To say hello from the other side!

Q: How do you organize
an astronomer's party?

A: You planet.

Q: When is a door not
really a door?

A: When it's really ajar.

I'D TELL YOU THE JOKE ABOUT
PERFORATED PAPER, BUT IT'S
TEAR-ABLE.

Q: WHAT DID EMINEM
SAY WHEN 50 CENT
MADE HIM SOME SOCKS?

A: "GEE, YOU KNIT?"

# Q: WHAT DID THE BUFFALO SAY WHEN HIS SON LEFT?

## A: BISON!

# Q: HOW DO YOU WEIGH A GEN X?

## A: IN INSTAGRAMS.

I WATCHED A PROGRAM ABOUT
BEAVERS LAST NIGHT.

IT WAS THE BEST DAM
PROGRAM I'VE EVER SEEN.

Q: WHY COULDN'T THE
BICYCLE STAND UP BY ITSELF?

A: IT WAS TOO TIRED.

DID YOU HEAR ABOUT THE
GUY WHO INVENTED THE
KNOCK KNOCK JOKE?

HE WON THE "NO-BELL"
PRIZE.

MY FAVORITE WORD IS
"DROOL"

IT JUST ROLLS OFF THE
TONGUE.

Q: What's the best thing about Switzerland?

A: I'm not sure, but the flag is a big plus.

Did you hear about the actor who fell through the floorboards?

Apparently, he was just going through a stage.

Q: Have you heard about the claustrophobic astronaut?

A: They say she just needs more space.

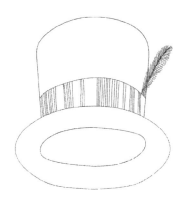

Q: Why is it impossible to explain puns to kleptomaniacs?

A: Because they always take things literally.

Q: What kind of exercise do lazy folk do?

A: Diddly-squats.

Q: What did the bald man say when his son gave him a comb as a gift?

A: Thanks, I'll never part with it!

Q: WHY DID THE OREO
BOOK AN EMERGENCY
DENTIST APPOINTMENT?

A: BECAUSE HE LOST HIS
FILLING.

Q: WHY DID THE NURSE
NEED A RED PEN AT WORK?

A: IN CASE THEY NEEDED
TO DRAW BLOOD.

THE STRANGEST THING
HAPPENED THIS MORNING,
I WENT TO THE PAPER SHOP...

AND IT HAD BLOWN AWAY.

DAD: YOUR MUM KNEW I WAS
A KEEPER AS SOON AS SHE MET
ME!
KID: HOW?
DAD: I WAS WEARING MASSIVE
GLOVES.

TWO PIECES OF TARMAC
ENTERED A BAR; THEY WERE
REALLY HARD CASES.
THEY HID UNDER THE TABLE
WHEN A RED PIECE OF
TARMAC CAME IN; HE WAS A
BIT OF A CYCLE PATH.

I WENT TO BUY SOME
CAMOUFLAGE PANTS THE
OTHER DAY,
BUT I COULDN'T FIND ANY.

I USED TO BE ADDICTED TO SOAP...

BUT I'M CLEAN NOW.

A BOOK JUST FELL ON MY HEAD.

I ONLY HAVE MY SHELF TO BLAME.

I HAVE BEEN DIAGNOSED AS
BEING COLOR BLIND.

IT HAS TOTALLY COME OUT
OF THE PURPLE.

WIFE: STOP TELLING
EXCEPTIONALLY BAD DAD
JOKES AND WRITE A BOOK
OR SOMETHING!
ME: WELL...THATS A
NOVEL IDEA.

If you have enjoyed this book of awful Dad jokes, I ask you kindly to please leave a review on Amazon. It has a significant impact on independent artists, authors & businesses.

Thanks a latte!

Made in the USA
Coppell, TX
08 December 2022

88114038R00062